THE OFFICIAL
LIVERPOOL FC
ANNUAL 2018

Designed by Chris Dalrymple

A Grange Publication

©2017. Published by Grange Communications Ltd., Edinburgh, under licence from The Liverpool Football Club and Athletic Grounds Ltd. Printed in the EU.

ISBN 978-1-911287-74-2

Contents

Honours List

League Champions
1900-01, 1905-06, 1921-22, 1922-23, 1946-47, 1963-64, 1965-66, 1972-73, 1975-76, 1976-77, 1978-79, 1979-80, 1981-82, 1982-83, 1983-84, 1985-86, 1987-88, 1989-90

European Cup Winners
1976-77, 1977-78, 1980-81, 1983-84, 2004-05

FA Cup Winners
1964-65, 1973-74, 1985-86, 1988-89, 1991-92, 2000-01, 2005-06

League Cup Winners
1980-81, 1981-82, 1982-83, 1983-84, 1994-95, 2000-01, 2002-03, 2011-12

UEFA Cup Winners
1972-73, 1975-76, 2000-01

European Super Cup Winners
1977, 2001, 2005

FA Charity Shield Winners
1964*, 1965*, 1966, 1974, 1976, 1977*, 1979, 1980, 1982, 1986*, 1988, 1989, 1990*, 2001, 2006 (*shared)

Super Cup Winners
1985-86

Division Two Winners
1893-94, 1895-96, 1904-05, 1961-62

Lancashire League Winners
1892-93

Reserve Division One Winners
1956-57, 1968-69, 1969-70, 1970-71, 1972-73, 1973-74, 1974-75, 1975-76, 1976-77, 1978-79, 1979-80, 1980-81, 1981-82, 1983-84, 1984-85, 1989-90, 1999-2000, 2007-08

FA Youth Cup Winners
1995-96, 2005-06, 2006-07

Season Review 2016/17

It may have lacked the drama of the previous season when it came to the cup competitions but 2016/17 was another season of significant progress for Liverpool, with a much-improved showing in the Premier League leading to a much-coveted place back among the European elite...

It all began on a sun-drenched afternoon in north London. Liverpool faced a tough opening, away to Arsenal, but showed their credentials by running out impressive 4-3 winners, with big summer signing Sadio Mané netting twice on his competitive debut.

It was a victory that sent expectations soaring and although a shock 2-0 reverse at newly promoted Burnley the following week momentarily doused the mood of optimism, a subsequent 15-game unbeaten run in league and cup saw it quickly rise once again.

September saw the official opening of the new Main Stand, an occasion commemorated with a resounding 4-1 success over reigning champions Leicester. Maximum points were then collected at Stamford Bridge, while Hull and Watford were beaten heavily at Anfield.

It was a run of form that took Liverpool to the Premier League summit and they remained there for a month until defensive errors led to a late collapse at Bournemouth in early December, when a seemingly comfortable 3-1 lead was surrendered.

As Christmas approached the Reds bounced back, Mané pounced to score a last-gasp winner in the Merseyside derby at Goodison Park, while another of the new recruits – Gini Wijnaldum, was the match-winner as the curtain came down on 2016 with another 1-0 win, at home to Manchester City.

It was not to be a happy New Year though. With man-of-the-moment Mané away representing Senegal at the African Cup of Nations, and Philippe Coutinho still not recovered from an injury sustained the previous month, Liverpool struggled.

A successive League Cup final appearance looked very much a possibility, with only Southampton standing in their way at the semi-final stage. Single goal defeats, home and away, in the two-legged tie put paid to aspirations of a return to Wembley in that competition and, three days later, Liverpool also exited the FA Cup, bowing out as victims of a giantkilling at Anfield – where they lost 2-1 to Championship side Wolves.

It left Klopp's men with just the Premier League to concentrate on. The title hopes that had burned brightly in the first half of the season, however, were all but extinguished following a dismal period in which Liverpool took just three points from 15 during the early weeks of 2017.

A much-coveted top four finish remained a realistic target and home victories over fellow challengers Tottenham and Arsenal boosted those chances. There was further cause for cheer when a derby double was completed over Everton but it was a failure to beat teams lower down the division that meant Liverpool's bid for Champions League qualification went down to the wire.

Thankfully, a strong finish ensured that the club's season-long goal was eventually achieved. On the penultimate weekend of the Premier League campaign an impressive 4-0 victory away to West Ham left the Reds in pole position to claim fourth place and, seven days later, a comfortable 3-0 home win over Middlesbrough did just that to round the season off on a high.

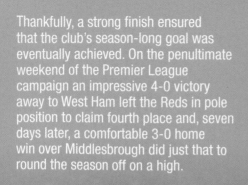

Date	Opponent		Competition	Score
14.08.2016	Arsenal	a	Premier League	4-3
20.08.2016	Burnley	a	Premier League	0-2
23.08.2016	Burton Albion	a	League Cup 2nd round	5-0
27.08.2016	Tottenham Hotspur	a	Premier League	1-1
10.09.2016	Leicester City	h	Premier League	4-1
16.09.2016	Chelsea	a	Premier League	2-1
20.09.2016	Derby County	a	League Cup 3rd round	3-0
24.09.2016	Hull City	h	Premier League	5-1
01.10.2016	Swansea City	a	Premier League	2-1
17.10.2016	Manchester United	h	Premier League	0-0
22.10.2016	West Bromwich Albion	h	Premier League	2-1
25.10.2016	Tottenham Hotspur	h	League Cup 4th round	2-1
29.10.2016	Crystal Palace	a	Premier League	4-2
06.11.2016	Watford	h	Premier League	6-1
19.11.2016	Southampton	a	Premier League	0-0
26.11.2016	Sunderland	h	Premier League	2-0
29.11.2016	Leeds United	h	League Cup 5th round	2-0
04.12.2016	Bournemouth	a	Premier League	3-4
11.12.2016	West Ham United	h	Premier League	2-2
14.12.2016	Middlesbrough	a	Premier League	3-0
19.12.2016	Everton	a	Premier League	1-0
27.12.2016	Stoke City	h	Premier League	4-1
31.12.2016	Manchester City	h	Premier League	1-0
02.01.2017	Sunderland	a	Premier League	2-2
08.01.2017	Plymouth Argyle	h	FA Cup 3rd round	0-0
11.01.2017	Southampton	a	League Cup Semi-final 1st leg	0-1
15.01.2017	Manchester United	a	Premier League	1-1
18.01.2017	Plymouth Argyle	a	FA Cup 3rd round replay	1-0
21.01.2017	Swansea City	h	Premier League	2-3
25.01.2017	Southampton	h	League Cup Semi-final 2nd leg	0-1
28.01.2017	Wolves	h	FA Cup 4th round	1-2
31.01.2017	Chelsea	h	Premier League	1-1
04.02.2017	Hull City	a	Premier League	0-2
11.02.2017	Tottenham Hotspur	h	Premier League	2-0
27.02.2017	Leicester City	a	Premier League	1-3
04.03.2017	Arsenal	h	Premier League	3-1
12.03.2017	Burnley	h	Premier League	2-1
19.03.2017	Manchester City	a	Premier League	1-1
01.04.2017	Everton	h	Premier League	3-1
05.04.2017	Bournemouth	h	Premier League	2-2
08.04.2017	Stoke City	a	Premier League	2-1
16.04.2017	West Bromwich Albion	a	Premier League	1-0
23.04.2017	Crystal Palace	h	Premier League	1-2
01.05.2017	Watford	a	Premier League	1-0
07.05.2017	Southampton	h	Premier League	0-0
14.05.2017	West Ham United	a	Premier League	4-0
21.05.2017	Middlesbrough	h	Premier League	3-0

Player debuts

- Sadio Mané against Arsenal on 14.08.2016
- Ragnar Klavan against Arsenal on 14.08.2016
- Georginio Wijnaldum against Arsenal on 14.08.2016
- Marko Grujić against Burnley on 20.08.2016
- Joël Matip against Burton Albion on 23.08.2016
- Loris Karius against Derby on 20.09.2016
- Ovie Ejaria against Derby on 20.09.2016
- Trent Alexander-Arnold against Tottenham on 25.10.2016
- Ben Woodburn against Sunderland on 26.11.2016
- Harry Wilson against Plymouth Argyle on 18.01.2017

Game Stats

- Total games: 47
- Games won: 27
- Games drawn: 11
- Games lost: 9
- Clean sheets - league: 12
- Clean sheets - overall: 17
- Total goals: 92
- Average attendance at home - league: 50,308
- Average attendance at home - overall: 50,763
- Average goals per game - League: 2.37
- Average goals per game - Overall: 2.08
- Average goal minute - League: 47
- Average goal minute - Overall: 47

Goal minutes

- Goals from 1 to 15: 7
- Goals from 16 to 30: 19
- Goals from 31 to 45: 18
- Goals from 46 to 60: 20
- Goals from 61 to 75: 16
- Goals from 76 to 90: 12
- Goals from 91 to 120: 0

Goals split down to competitions

- England Premier League - 78
- League Cup - 12
- FA Cup - 2

Klopp-Talkin'

After completing his first full season in the Anfield hot-seat, manager Jürgen Klopp took stock and reflected on what had been another eventful campaign for the Reds…

Turning doubters into believers

"You win at Arsenal, it was outstanding, then you play Burnley, you lose it and nobody said it was a slip. Immediately everybody said, "That always happens to us", [we] win such a big game and lose against a smaller side. To lose is already hard enough but to have the feeling "That's our DNA", it's really sad, how can we change this? People said when we didn't beat the weaker teams that I have no Plan B. I have absolutely no problem, people can say what they want, but it's not about Plan B. We know exactly what to do, we did it so often. When we did it, it's normal, when we didn't do it, it's like we'll never learn it! [But] we scored the fourth most, only a few teams scored more than we did. It was all good."

Mixed fortunes at the turn of the year

"It's unbelievable when you think at the end of the year, Manchester City, what a game [from] both sides. Running, good football, defending together, tactically good - what a commercial for football. Only one goal, but a commercial for football. Two days later, it felt like another kind of sport. Going to Sunderland, two penalties for them, a handball of Sadio - it was handball but nobody, Sadio included, could explain why he did it. In this moment, this club and this city maybe, we have to learn to take moments like this like they are. Don't make them bigger. [At Liverpool], we are like, if you win against Manchester City the world could not be nicer, you draw at Sunderland and everything is terrible and that's the start of something bad. Yes, it was not good, [but] we missed players, players came back who were not in shape, we all know."

Bouncing back from a poor run of form

"In life, you cannot ignore the negative things that have happened. If you can change them, change them; if you can't change them, ignore them. That's how it is. You cannot go [back] so it's not about negative experiences, we all have them, it's all about the reaction. That's life and that's football - how you react on a specific case. Your normal day: if you get up in the morning and the first hour is bad, does that mean go back to bed? No, it means let's try another one. That's football, it's the same, only we do it with 10 other people on a pitch, millions of people watching it. It looks like it makes it more important because we cannot hide but, in the end, we have to do the same things as anyone else, we have to react on things in the best way."

The pressure of chasing Champions League qualification

"The last three or four weeks were difficult because we were always five/six/seven points ahead but [Arsenal and Manchester United] had all the games in hand. Watching it and not hoping that they lose is, for a human being, quite difficult. I don't want that somebody loses but in this moment we can say, "Come on, the other team win"! From a human perspective, that's how it is. We needed to learn not to watch football in the week and hope that something happened. We had to stick to what we knew - playing football, winning the games, and seeing what it led us to. That's what we did from a specific point and it was easier to do it again."

The opening goal vs. 'Boro on the final day and clinching a top four finish

"I can't 100 per cent say exactly what I felt in this moment because if I could judge how I celebrated then it would be completely different. I saw the game back again and I saw my celebration obviously and I would say it was a big relief. Over the season - I know we have red-tinted glasses, but we leave them away - there was not a lot of luck, that's how it was. You really want [to be able] to go through this and get something at the end of the season. And that's what we did, actually. We spoke about the things we couldn't have influence on but there are, of course, a few things we could have influence on. [The goal] was the moment when you see that's the final step we had to do this season, to open this game, because it was clear then with the qualities of the boys that it would be done. It was a big moment."

The future

"I know that we are good already but we have so much space to improve - I love it. Being really good and feeling there's not a lot more possible, that's still OK but you think how can you keep this? We can really improve. That's what I'm really looking forward to. We have to, obviously, because around us we have a lot but we will really be a challenger, we will fight. We will play good football on the good days, on the less good days we will still fight for the result. I really feel positive. I'm really optimistic for our future, not because I'm crazy but only because I know what we have, I know what we will get, I know what we can get, and I know that we really have a super bunch of people - knowledge, character - not just the players, all around."

Home Comforts

We take a sneak peak inside the new home dressing room at Anfield...

It may have been one of the last areas of the new Main Stand to be completed but - judging by these pictures – for Jürgen Klopp, his coaching staff and the players, it was certainly worth the wait.

In April 2017 the doors opened on an ultra-spacious, brand-new, home dressing room. After being forced to change in a makeshift space since the demolition of the old stand it must have been a very welcoming sight for the team.

This state-of-the-art area, which has been designed to mirror the facilities at the club's Melwood training ground, features contemporary decor while also remaining in-keeping with Anfield's traditional style.

Other design features include name plates over each of the players' changing positions in the famous Liverpool red and a fully-equipped warm-up and treatment room with the latest 4G artificial turf.

A dressing room is one of the most important areas in any football stadium and it's clear to see that the club can now boast a facility worthy of the world-class talent that use it.

Situated deep in the bowels of the Main Stand, it was christened in style when used for the first time on April Fools' Day. Everton provided the opposition in a Premier League fixture that afternoon and Liverpool ran out 3-1 winners.

Let's hope it will host many more post-match celebrations in years to come.

Player Profiles

Simon Mignolet

Goalkeeper

Squad Number: 22

Loris Karius

Goalkeeper

Squad Number: 1

Nathaniel Clyne

Defender

Squad Number: 2

Andrew Robertson

Defender

Squad Number: 26

Four Supporters, Four Stories, Pure Liverpool

To help launch Liverpool's home kit for the 2017/18 season, four unsuspecting supporters were treated to a special surprise.

Charlie Gallagher, Andrew Ward, Robbie Fowler and Max Dutton are fanatical fans who embody what it means to be Pure Liverpool FC.

So, ahead of the kit's official release, as a reward for their loyalty to the club, each was given a sneak preview of the shirt by one of their heroes.

These are their stories...

"My name is Charlie Gallagher. I was born on 20 May 1922. I have a season ticket and go to every home game. I came out of the army in 1946 and started going to watch Liverpool at the beginning of the fifties, well before the glory years. My sons started going and then my grandsons. We always talk about football and how Liverpool are playing. We've had our ups and downs but you've still got to support the team. Going to the football and watching Liverpool play, winning the cups and winning the leagues, it's just part of your life."

"This is my son Andrew [Ward] and LFC is his life. From the age of about six or seven he used to go with his dad to every game. He absolutely loved the atmosphere and the excitement. He was knocked down just before he was 14. And then he lost his season ticket because he was comatose for a long time. Graeme Souness was manager at the time and Graeme used to come in unannounced, late at night, and sit and talk to him. I promised Andrew, if he came out of this for us, I would take him to every game. When we got the season ticket it changed his life immensely and, honestly, for us to go as a family is unbelievable."

"My name is Robbie Fowler. I've been going to the match for 12 or 13 years now. I travel up from Stafford, where I live, for every home game. The stresses and strains of work are all worth it when you see the lads go out for 90 minutes. It is very much a release. The people I've met through going to the game have become my closest friends. I've got a lot to thank this football club for, and the values that it represents echo what I believe in my life. When you're in that ground you can be yourself. You're surrounded by likeminded people. It's one of the best feelings in the world. I'm so lucky that I get to do it."

"My name is Max Dutton and I am seven years old. I support Liverpool and I love Liverpool. I started supporting Liverpool because of my dad but I would have supported them anyway because they are the best. I like it when my dad takes me to the match because you get to see the players actually playing, rather than just on TV. My favourite players are Mané, Coutinho and Firmino. Coutinho always scores and does the assists to help us score. I love it when he scores because it helps the team and it's fun scoring. The best thing about Philippe Coutinho is that he does boss goals."

Training: The Liverpool Way

It's at Liverpool's training complex in West Derby where the players are put through their paces in preparation for a matchday. But what actually goes on behind the gates of Melwood as a big game looms? First team coach Peter Krawietz explains how a typical week of training is planned and executed...

"Training is a mixture between hard work and fun - but work is the most important [thing] for us, always focused and always concentrated during these 90 minutes every day.

"We try to improve our players and we try to improve our team. We always think, and we are completely convinced, that you can get better with good training.

"To stay physically strong, to get stronger, to work on your tactical ideas, to work on your technical skills – we try to always put this in every day. Everything we do follows an idea and a target: to get better, to play better football.

"You try to bring the players to a certain level physically and then you have to watch week by week by week, every week, what happened in the game.

"What do we need the next time? What do we have to change? What do we have to improve? Is it the defence? Is it the attack? Most of the time it's both! It's never boring.

"Maybe the exercises are similar, but you always have different points in a special way where you can improve. So even after the best game, we never say it's not possible to be better. We always keep improving and keep going."

"Every session is different. It depends which day of the week we are on.

"With a match on a Saturday, we will have a training session on Sunday morning where the players who played 90 minutes will have recovery and the players who didn't play will have a 'load', as we say, so they train in the same way as for a major game with small games. For them, it's a little harder.

"If we have a long week then Monday is off. On Tuesday morning, we start with stability training, so it's physical and a few passing exercises. Tuesday is the day with two training sessions – in the afternoon, again starting the week by playing small games.

"Wednesday is the session where we start the special preparation for the next game on Saturday, with a unit 11v11 – not a full game, of course, but finding different situations where we simulate the 11v11 on the whole pitch.

"On Thursday, we continue to prepare the game, especially with finishing exercises – shooting on goal, playing crosses, with a tactical background.

"Friday's session, the last before the game, we train set-pieces and the famous game in our squad: old vs. young. It's a competition over the whole season, where it's always the 11 youngest against the 11 oldest. Then we are prepared, in most cases, for the game."

19

Countdown to Kick-Off with
Gini Wijnaldum

The Reds number five talks us through his usual routine as he prepares for matchday…

When it begins…

"By the time we reach the middle of the week, it's all about looking to the next game. Of course, as football players, you will always look back at the last game because you take the good things to give you confidence and the bad things to change them into good things. You want to learn from the mistakes you've made and you want to take the good things you did with you. I am always looking forward in life, but with a few things from the past that I can do better or take with me. Sometimes in training, you will look at things that maybe didn't go so well in the previous game; you'll work on it, improve it and take it into the next game."

Training…

"We always train to do good things in the game. If we can hurt a team with counter-pressing, for example, we'll train all week on this. As soon as we begin training again after recovery, we will look forward and think about how we can hurt our opponent. Training here is quite intense because of the way we want to play, counter-pressing and a lot of running, positional play and so on. You have to be fit and train hard to stay fit, otherwise you will find it difficult in games. It's a good thing and I like to play like that with that dominance."

Analysing the opposition…

"We always respect the opposition in our preparations, but it's about what we can do. That's what the manager is always telling us. Of course, you have to be aware about the things the opponent can do well and the things we need to be ready for, but the manager says if we do all the things right, we can make them do those things they do well less. He always looks at us first before he looks at the opponents – that's how I like it and that's how it has to be when you play for a team like Liverpool. We play with a lot of good players here, so we must first look at our qualities and then the quality of the opponent."

Rest & relaxation…

"We always stay in a hotel the night before a game. In the beginning, that was a little bit strange for me because in all the previous clubs I'd been at, we'd never stayed in hotels the night before home matches, just away games. It meant I could stay with my family and sleep in my own bed, but now having done it, I think staying in hotels before games is a good thing. It helps you get really focused, no-one is bothering you, you can chill out the way you want and you're with the team. So now I am used to doing that and think it's a really good thing, both for us as players and as a team.

"You can take your PlayStation with you, everything that helps you to relax. Personally I watch TV shows on my laptop, or movies. I also like to listen to music to relax in my hotel room, a lot of Dutch music as well as Rap, Hip-Hop and RnB. I think Drake is now the rapper of the moment. I listen to him a lot"

Matchday…

"I look to get up at nine o'clock on matchdays, even if it's an evening game because we train in the morning. On those days, we'll then go back to the hotel, sleep, get up again and prepare for the game. So, it's always nine o'clock for me. I'll also pray before matches in the morning when I get up. That's my only pre-match ritual.

"I am always feeling relaxed on the day of a game. I am going to play a game and I am going to try and enjoy it. I think it's just my personality; I want to enjoy the game and make the best of it. I've always been that way. I don't get nervous about matches – in fact, I have more nerves about games involving my former clubs! When two of my old teams played against each other – Feyenoord and PSV – I had more nerves for that game than our game that weekend. I don't know why… they're just two of my old teams and I support them."

Pre-match meals

"What I eat on matchday depends on how I feel that day. In the morning, I will eat bread with strawberry jam, or bread and eggs, or omelette, or porridge. I try not to eat a lot in the mornings because if I do, I will stay full and that makes it harder for me to eat a pre-match meal in the afternoon. I have learned in my career, you have to find out what's the best way for you personally to prepare for a game – and I realised it was better for me to have a small breakfast and then eat in the afternoon, a few hours before the game instead of a lot in the morning and not much in the afternoon. It's about having energy. In the afternoon, we will have pasta, rice, chicken, salads, fruit… again; you can choose what you want."

In the dressing room…

"The atmosphere is good in the dressing room before a game. Really good. Everyone is busy with making himself ready for the game. A few guys will go to the treatment room, a few guys will do exercises in order for their body to be ready for the game, but otherwise the players will just sit in their place and listen to music and so on. I like to have a massage for games to get myself ready."

Final thoughts…

"When we're lined up in the tunnel, I'm not really thinking anything other than 'We're about to play a game'. When we're at home and you hear 'You'll Never Walk Alone', that's still something that's really good to hear. I am always happy when I hear it – it still gives me goose bumps. It's different playing here as a Liverpool player, knowing they're all on your side. It gives you a great feeling."

Goal of the Season 2016/17

A countdown of the ten best Liverpool goals scored during the 2016/17 season…

1 Emre Can v Watford (a) 1 May 2017

2 Jordan Henderson v Chelsea (a) 16 September 2016

3 Roberto Firmino v Stoke City (a) 8 April 2017

4 Sadio Mané v Arsenal (a) 14 August 2016

5 Philippe Coutinho v Everton (h) 1 April 2017

Roberto Firmino v Swansea City (h) 21 January 2017 **7**

Philippe Coutinho v Arsenal (a) 14 August 2016 **6**

8 Divock Origi v Middlesbrough (a) 14 December 2016

Emre Can v Burnley (h) 12 March 2017 **9**

10 Gini Wijnaldum v Manchester City (h) 31 December 2016

23

Player Profiles

Alberto Moreno
Defender
Squad Number: 18

Dejan Lovren
Defender
Squad Number: 6

Joël Matip

Defender

Squad Number: 32

Ragnar Klavan

Defender

Squad Number: 17

Legends Turn Out For Charity

A sell-out Anfield crowd were treated to a thrilling blast from the past on 25 March 2017 as a star-studded array of Liverpool and Real Madrid legends rolled back the years in the name of charity.

On what was a free weekend of domestic football due to the international break, 54,000 got their 'footy fix' and more, as they turned up to see some of the biggest names of the past two decades pull on their boots once again.

The game was played in aid of the Liverpool FC Foundation and among the star men on show for the Reds were five of the 2005 Champions League winning team, including Steven Gerrard and Jamie Carragher, as well as the likes of Robbie Fowler, Michael Owen and Steve McManaman.

Lining up on the opposite side were such luminaries as Luis Figo, Roberto Carlos, Clarence Seedoorf and

Emilio Butragueño, while former Liverpool and Real striker Fernando Morientes also featured.

When the two teams met at the Bernabeu in 2015 it was Los Blancos who ran out 4-2 winners but it was the Reds who triumphed on this occasion.

Steven Gerrard was in fine form as he set up goals for Owen and John Aldridge, then won a penalty which Fowler converted, before getting on the scoresheet himself to give Liverpool a seemingly unassailable 4-0 lead with just 12 minutes remaining.

A late rally by the visitors saw them respond with three quick-fire goals, including one from Morientes, but it wasn't enough and the Liverpool Legends gained some revenge for the defeat two years earlier.

More importantly, a great day was had by all and a significant amount of funding was raised. Andrea Cooper, head of the LFC Foundation, said: "I would like to thank everyone who supported this game – our supporters, the legends, our charity matchday sponsors, the club and all our staff. This helped us to deliver a truly fantastic day to remember at Anfield and raise a huge amount of money."

Realmadrid
Leyendas

Liverpool Legends

Dudek
Westerveld
Henchoz
Kennedy
Kvarme
McAteer
Agger
Babb
Riise
McManaman
Aldridge
Gerrard
Rush
Fowler (c)
García
Owen
Šmicer
Diao
Hamann
McAllister
Carragher
Thompson

Real Madrid Legends

Contreras
Salgado
Carlos
Pavón
Llorente
Butragueño
McManaman
Morientes
Figo
Seedorf
Owen
De la Red
Bortolini
Amavisca
Sánchez (GK)
Congo
Karembeu
Velasco
Sanz

Lucas
10 Years A Red

Before leaving for Lazio in the summer of 2017, Lucas Leiva became the first South American to complete a decade of service at Liverpool and before joining up with his new club he sat down to reminisce about some of the major moments and key figures during his life with the Reds…

Rafa
"He had a big influence in me moving to Liverpool. I was going to play for a top manager at a top club, it was everything that I wanted for the next step in my career. I'll always be grateful to Rafa and what he did for me."

First game (28 August 2007)
"It was the Champions League qualifier against Toulouse. I got a very good reception. We won 4-0 and got through to the group stage. It was brilliant."

Derby debut (20 October 2007)
"I could see the reaction of the fans as I replaced Stevie, nobody really understood it. But, in the end, it worked out well. We won the game and I almost scored the winner. The celebrations with the fans afterwards helped me understand just what this game means."

Gerrard, Alonso, Mascherano and Sissoko
"We had a top class midfield and breaking into that was a big challenge for me. I realised I had to be patient. I had to watch these players and learn. Thankfully, Rafa always put a lot of trust in me. He could see me every day in training, trying to get better."

First goal (26 January 2008)
"I'd scored a few in training that week and this was very similar. We were losing the game so it came at a good time. I was the first Brazilian to score for Liverpool so it's a nice memory and we ended up winning the game quite easily."

Early doubts
"To be honest, I felt like it wasn't going well. My first year here was really hard, adapting to a new league and a different language. I played a fair few games but not as many as I'd have liked and my future at the club was in a little bit of doubt."

Seeing Red at Goodison (4 February 2009)
"It felt like something was always against me to succeed at Liverpool. It was an FA Cup replay and I got sent-off. To make matters worse Everton went on to score in the last minute of extra-time and knock us out. At that moment I probably thought I wouldn't play for Liverpool again."

2009/10
"I think this was the season that things started to turn for me. I played a lot of games and although we finished badly in the league, for me, it was a fantastic season on a personal level and to be voted Young Player of the Season by the fans put a smile on my face."

King Kenny
"When Kenny came, he was fantastic with me. He just gave me all the confidence I needed to go and play and show my skill. We ended the season on a high and I finished very strong as well. It was probably the first year that I went home on holiday to Brazil with my mind a little bit more positive about my future for the club."

Completing a decade with the Reds
"To be playing here for 10 years is a massive achievement for me. I'm really proud. It seems that it's a long time but, to be honest, it has gone very quickly. Of course in difficult moments, it goes a little bit slower. But, overall, it has been very positive – I have learned a lot and improved as a player and a person. Liverpool is a family club. I feel I have made many friends and people that will be part of my life forever."

Injured at Stamford Bridge (29 November 2011)
"We'd played just 48 hours earlier and Kenny made a lot of changes. But I pushed to play in this game. I was on a fantastic run of form and receiving praise from everywhere, something that I wasn't used to. We were 2-0 up and I felt something in my knee but at that moment I never knew it would be that bad."

2013/14
"It was a fantastic season. We had that crazy run. Winning games, scoring goals and getting results nobody expected – like against Everton, Arsenal and Manchester United. We really thought that we were going to do it. But in the end it just didn't happen. It was really sad. We were close but it wasn't enough."

Wecome Back
Stevie G

A familiar face returned to Liverpool Football Club in 2017 and he was welcomed back with open arms.

Just two years after calling time on his illustrious playing career at Anfield, club legend Steven Gerrard opened a new chapter in his long association with the Reds.

Following a brief stint Stateside, playing for LA Galaxy in the MLS, Gerrard came back to his spiritual home to take up a coaching role at the Liverpool Academy.

On the first day of February Gerrard officially began work at the youth training base in Kirkby, initially operating in a wide-ranging role in the professional development phase of the young players, and his inspirational presence around the place was quickly felt.

Just two months later it was announced that come the 2017/18 season Gerrard would take charge of Liverpool's under-18 team and those lucky enough to have already benefitted from Gerrard's wealth of knowledge and experience will testify that his appointment represents an exciting new era at the Academy.

He rose through the youth ranks of Liverpool himself, graduating to the first team as an 18-year old before writing his name indelibly into Kop folklore as one of the greatest players ever to pull on the famous red shirt.

After 710 appearances, 186 goals and 10 trophies, including that never-to-be-forgotten Champions League triumph in 2005, Steven Gerrard's work at the club he loves is not done yet...

Describe how it felt returning to Liverpool…

"There were a few nerves there, more excitement really. [It was] nothing like the nerves compared to your debut where you feel that sort of scared feeling. Knowing I was going back to work for the club again was a big buzz and it's something that was always on my mind from the day I left. I knew that one day I would represent the club again. I didn't know how long that was going to be but I think the club made the transition pretty smooth and quick. They were on the phone to me towards the end of my playing career and said they wanted me back to work for the club, which is fantastic for me and my family."

Was it about convincing yourself you could make an impact as a coach?

"Those feelings are still there now because I still don't know whether I'm going to be a top coach. Nobody knows just yet, I'm still learning, I'm right at the beginning of the journey. I feel confident and I feel like I've got a fantastic load of knowledge from being a player and being around top managers and coaches. But it's very, very early - it's my first job."

What advice have you been given?

"How it is similar to being a player as in you get out of it what you put in. I always had that motto when I was a player. If you work hard on the training pitch and you learn, and you're like a sponge, it certainly helps you as a footballer. If I can do that as a coach, put the hours in on the training pitch and also do my own work off it, and be around top coaches, I can only get better."

What was your reaction to being appointed manager of Liverpool under-18s?

"It's a fantastic feeling. Obviously, I was very happy and delighted to be back working for the club, but to get the role of U18s manager, it's a big gig and I'm really excited and looking forward to it."

You set high standards as a player… will it be the same as a coach?

"I don't think it'll change, I'm committed, I want this, I know the hours are longer and whatever! I'm up for it; I'm up for the challenge. I haven't set myself any targets, I'm just going to take each day as it comes and try and learn and become the best coach I can."

What sort of relationship have you struck up with Alex Inglethorpe?

"I already had a really good relationship with Alex, he used to come down and spend time at Melwood under Brendan, he'd always be popping in and out. I always had a decent relationship with him but since I've gone in, I couldn't have asked him for any more, really, he's been absolutely first class with me. We have regular talks and chats, he knows what my plan is, where I want to get to and what I want to be, and I think he's a fantastic mentor for me. Having Steve Heighway there as well, and all the other coaches, we're quite blessed at the Academy, there are some really top coaches down there."

You had first-team offers from other clubs before re-joining Liverpool…

"The key thing about this is [that] it's Liverpool U18s, it's massive, but it's away from the cameras. I know I'm going to make loads of mistakes, that's part of the process. One of the things Jürgen said to me when I sat down with

him [was], 'You'll make mistakes, you've got to learn from them, grow and move on - and you ideally want to do that away from cameras'. Now, the U18s get a little bit of exposure, and I'm sure people are going to be looking out for results and seeing how I'm doing, which is fine because you obviously still need to have a little bit of exposure. In terms of the other jobs that were offered to me before I decided to come back to the club, they were all too early."

What are the links like between the Academy and first team?

"Pep Lijnders is a great coach, I think we're lucky to have him. The boys go down to Melwood and have a session with Pep once a week, which I think is fantastic for them. We're blessed and, as I say, we've also got a manager who's very open and very supportive of the Academy. I think he was more excited than me as the chats progressed and, when he thought about me coming back and being manager of the U18s, he was super excited. He's been first class."

What does success look like for you?

"Having a successful team – results. It doesn't matter what game or sport you're involved in, if you're a coach, you're going to get judged on results. We have to try and win and play good football because that's what's demanded at Liverpool Football Club."

Competition

Answer the following question correctly and you could win a signed Liverpool FC shirt.

Q Which club did Jürgen Klopp manage prior to joining Liverpool?

A. Manchester United
B. Borussia Dortmund
C. FC Barcelona

Entry is by email only. Only one entry per contestant. Please enter LFC SHIRT followed by either A, B or C in the subject line of an email. In the body of the email, please include your full name, address, postcode, email address and phone number and send to: frontdesk@grangecommunications.co.uk by Friday 30th March 2018.

Last year's winner Alexander with his signed shirt!

Terms and Conditions

1) The closing date for this competition is Friday the 30th March 2018 at midnight. Entries received after that time will not be counted.

2) Information on how to enter and on the prizes form part of these conditions.

3) Entry is open to those residing in the UK only. If entrants are under 18, consent from a parent or guardian must be obtained and the parent or guardian must agree to these terms and conditions.

4) This competition is not open to employees or their relatives of Liverpool FC. Any such entries will be invalid.

5) The start date for entries is 31st October 2017 at 4pm.

6) Entries must be strictly in accordance with these terms and conditions. Any entry not in strict accordance with these terms and conditions will be deemed to be invalid and no prizes will be awarded in respect of such entry. By entering, all entrants will be deemed to accept these rules.

7) One (1) lucky winner will win a 2017/2018 season signed football shirt.

8) The prize is non-transferable and no cash alternative will be offered. Entry is by email only. Only one entry per contestant. Please enter LFC SHIRT followed by either A, B or C in the subject line of an email. In the body of the email, please include your full name, address, postcode, email address and phone number and send to: frontdesk@ grangecommunications.co.uk by Friday 30th March 2018.

9) The winner will be picked at random. The winner will be contacted within 72 hours of the closing date. Details of the winners can be requested after this time from the address below.

10) Entries must not be sent in through agents or third parties. No responsibility can be accepted for lost, delayed, incomplete, or for electronic entries or winning notifications that are not received or delivered. Any such entries will be deemed void.

11) The winners shall have 72 hours to claim their prize once initial contact has been made by the Promoter. Failure to respond may result in forfeiture of the prize.

12) On entering the competition you are allowing Liverpool Football Club and its trusted partners to contact you with information about products and services they believe might be of interest to you. If you do not wish to receive any marketing information from the Club, you can opt out by emailing LFC STOP to frontdesk@grangecommunications.co.uk before midnight on Friday 30th March 2018.

13) The Promoter reserves the right to withdraw or amend the promotion as necessary due to circumstances outside its reasonable control. The Promoter's decision on all matters is final and no correspondence will be entered into.

14) The Promoter (or any third party nominated by the Promoter) may use the winner's name and image and their comments relating to the prize for future promotional, marketing and publicity purposes in any media worldwide without notice or without any fee being paid.

15) Liverpool Football Club's decision is final, no correspondence will be entered in to. Except in respect of death or personal injury resulting from any negligence of the Club, neither The Liverpool Football Club nor any of its officers, employees or agents shall be responsible for (whether in tort, contract or otherwise):

(i) any loss, damage or injury to you and/or any guest or to any property belonging to you or any guest in connection with this competition and/or the prize, resulting from any cause whatsoever;

(ii) for any loss of profit, loss of use, loss of opportunity or any indirect, economic or consequential losses whatsoever;

16) This competition shall be governed by English law.

17) Promoter: Grange Communications, 22 Great King Street, Edinburgh EH3 6QH.

Player Profiles

James Milner
Midfielder
Squad Number: 7

Georginio Wijnaldum
Midfielder
Squad Number: 5

Emre Can
Midfielder
Squad Number: 23

Marko Grujič
Midfielder
Squad Number: 16

Wordsearch

The names of 20 Liverpool captains (listed below) are hidden in this grid. Search horizontally, vertically or diagonally, forwards or backwards, to find them…

```
S V K N I H U G H E S D A K
M R F C R N S G C Y R L I W
I C K T E S C U L M T L P H
T L L P E B T E R L H E Y E
H Z P N Q J S H W G R D Y L
N H U R Y N W I O G D D H A
T O N E E R D H A M R I M N
S Y A S I C R P K R P L T F
G T N G M S A N N T Q S D M
S A H T E Y R N E A L H O M
H T R N B R R E L W O F K N
F T R S G R E D K N A P P G
G A U F J Z G K F R T K K B
B B V T Q N O S R E D N E H
```

Souness	Raisbeck	Whelan	Ince	Henderson
Hughes	Liddell	Wright	Barnes	Hyypia
Thompson	Busby	Fowler	Redknapp	Gerrard
Smith	Neal	Rush	Yeats	Hansen

Answers on page 60 & 61.

Colour in MIGHTY RED

40 YEARS
OF KING KENNY

10 August 2017 marked the 40th anniversary of a signing that is widely regarded as the greatest in Liverpool's history. 'King' Kenny Dalglish is one of the Reds' finest ever players and most successful managers. Four decades since first joining, he continues to serve the club in an ambassadorial role and remains a much-revered Anfield icon…

What are your first memories of Liverpool?

I first came to Liverpool when I was 15-years-old. I came down here on trial with a few boys from Scotland. I was asked to sign, but at 15 I felt a wee bit too young to be moving so far from home. When they [Liverpool] came in for me again, 11 years later, it was a no brainer for me to move here. There are not many people who get asked twice so I was very fortunate. The people made you feel very comfortable in and around the football club and the city of Liverpool made us feel very welcome as well. Coming from Glasgow I think it's [Liverpool] very similar. They had the shipyards, which were both very active at that time, they had people whose humour and commitment was the same, and two high profile football clubs that shared a great rivalry, so it was almost like just moving down the road a bit for me.

Can you describe what your relationship has been like with the fans over the years?

They've always been fantastically supportive, on and off the pitch. I think the greatest thing Liverpool have is that everybody is important – whether you are a supporter, a player or you worked at the club – everybody has a role to play. The supporters were always there to help us and we were there to help them. If we played well and won the game then brilliant. Everybody appreciated and respected each other and the role they played in the success of the football club. This was ultimately very important for me.

Tell us what it was like to score in front of the Kop…

If I'd had a good education I would be able to explain it for you! I think you can see in the faces of the Liverpool players who score in front of the Kop, how elated they are. What's important though is how they share that joy with everybody and don't keep it to themselves. For us it was always apparent that when we scored that most of the players came up to celebrate with you. We celebrated on the pitch but the celebrations were also for people off the pitch. Everybody joined in.

You achieved so much as a player and manager with Liverpool, how do you reflect on those glory days?

They were fantastic [days], the camaraderie was fantastic. People kept saying what is the secret about Liverpool? But if there was a secret we never got told it! People used to come and watch training to try and find out what was happening. They always thought that Liverpool were hiding something but there was nothing hidden. I think the biggest thing was that everybody who worked for the club, in whatever capacity, was always very good at their job. And we never got carried away with the success that we had.

What would be the outstanding highlight of your time at the club?

We were fortunate that there were so many of them but the most poignant and most rewarding one, for me, was winning the FA Cup in 1989, the year of the Hillsborough tragedy. That was really important for everybody.

Your name has now been associated with Liverpool, both the club and the city, for four decades – how does that make you feel?

The past 40 years have been fantastic, for me and my family. For us, this is our home now. Both Marina and I are very proud to be Glaswegians, born and brought up there, but we are equally proud to be adopted Scousers as well. The past 40 years have passed in the blink of an eye really and it's nice when you look back because there have been so many happy times.

Finally, what does Liverpool Football Club mean to you?

Everything.

Kenny Dalglish Fact-file

Born: 4 March 1951
Signed: 10 August 1977 (from Celtic)
Games: 515
Goals: 172
Management Years: 1985 to 1991 & 2011 to 2012

Honours Won
(as player and manager)

European Cup: 1978, 1981, 1984
League Championship: 1978/79, 1979/80, 1981/82, 1982/83, 1983/84, 1985/86, 1987/88, 1989/90
FA Cup: 1986, 1989
League Cup: 1981, 1982, 1983, 1984, 2011
European Super Cup: 1977
Charity Shield: 1977, 1979, 1980, 1982, 1986, 1988, 1989, 1990
Screensport Super Cup: 1986
FWA Player of the Year: 1979, 1983
PFA Player of the Year: 1983
Manager of the Year: 1986, 1988, 1990

Oh Mané, Mané

Sadio Mané was a proud recipient of the two main prizes at Liverpool Football Club's 2017 Players' Awards ceremony.

Mané, a summer 2016 recruit from Southampton capped an outstanding first campaign at the club by scooping both the Player of the Season, as voted for by supporters on the club website, and Players' Player of the Season accolades.

Despite being absent from the team during January because of his involvement at the African Cup of Nations and then being side-lined by injury since April, the Senegal international scored 13 goals in 29 appearances and brought an exciting mix of pace and creativity to the side.

He made an immediate impression on his fellow team-mates and became a firm fan favourite, with a last-gasp winner at Goodison Park being one of his many highlights.

"It is a big honour for me to win these trophies, especially with all of the great players in the dressing room," said Mané. "I want to thank everybody. I'm very happy. I have been learning a lot from the manager, the coaches and my teammates. That's been the key."

Other major winners on the night were Trent Alexander Arnold who scooped the Young Player of the Season award and Ben Woodburn who walked away with the Academy Players' Player of the Season.

Lucas Leiva collected a Special Recognition Award for completing a decade of service with the Reds, while Liverpool legend 'Sir' Roger Hunt - the club's all-time record league goalscorer - picked up the Lifetime Achievement Award. And 40 years after becoming the first team to bring the European Cup back to Anfield, the heroes of Rome '77 were honoured with the Outstanding Team Achievement Award.

2017 LFC Players' Awards winners in full

Young Player of the Season – Trent Alexander-Arnold
Supporters Club of the Season – Cyprus
Staff Recognition Award – Disability support team
First Team Players' Player of the Season – Sadio Mané
Academy Players' Player of the Season – Ben Woodburn
Ladies Players' Player of the Season – Sophie Ingle
Bill Shankly Community Award – Jeremy Barnes
Outstanding Team Achievement Award – Rome 1977 team
Special Recognition Award – Lucas Leiva
Goal of the Season – Emre Can (see page 22)
Lifetime Achievement Award – Roger Hunt
Player of the Season – Sadio Mané

Meet Our New CEO
Peter Moore

Lifelong Liverpudlian Peter Moore officially took up his 'dream' position as Liverpool FC's new chief executive officer in June 2017. Having previously held senior positions at Electronic Arts, Microsoft, Sega and Reebok, he brings a wealth of experience with him to what is a very important role…

How does it feel to be here in your position as Liverpool's chief executive officer?

"It's an honour, it's a privilege. As a lad from Liverpool, growing up I never would have dreamt that I'd be in a position to help and support the club, and guide us through what I think is going to be an incredibly exciting couple of years to come here. I think about my upbringing, I think about my love for this club and my experience in business, and being able to bring that together to help this club is unbelievable."

Is this unlike any position that you've held before, because of the emotional connection?

"It is. The emotional connection of not only the passion I have for the business of football, but this is my club. The great companies I've worked with before, I have a passion – a passion for the product, the brand and the people. But when you add the passion for your club, this is where I was born, this is very special. The weight of what I will be doing, on the expectations of hundreds of millions of people like me – devout Reds – it's huge for me."

You have worked for many years in an industry – gaming – that is forever evolving and changing. Do you expect to encounter similarities in football?

"At Electronic Arts, my most recent company, we enjoyed having over 300million players who interacted with us. I think Liverpool has huge similarities – hundreds of millions of people self-identify 'I'm a Liverpool fan.' We need to take the excitement that only 54,000 people can experience here and we need to globalise that. As a fan who lived 5,200 miles away, I soaked up the news. Who is going to play? Who is hurt? What formation is Jürgen going to put on the field? What's happening at Melwood today? Reaching out that way to fans, like myself, all around the world is very, very important."

Tell us about your remit and what you'll be responsible for…

"In broad terms, Jürgen, his coaching staff and the scouting teams are responsible for everything down there – success, goals, clean sheets and entertaining football. Giving the fans who come here and watch all around the world everything they deserve. In my world, my team and my remit is to provide all of the resources, the support, the revenue required. Football is big business nowadays. This club deserves and is determined to be where we were in the '70s and '80s as a world-class club and, in my estimation, the best club in the world. We have the best footballing story, we're the biggest footballing family in the world. My job is to make sure we deliver against everything that I as a fan, I as the CEO and everybody that loves what we do here, deliver against their expectations."

Quiz is Anfield

How strong is your knowledge of the Reds? This is your chance to put it to the test…

Last Season

1. Against which club did Ben Woodburn score his first senior Liverpool goal?

2. Who returned to the club as an Academy coach?

3. What was Liverpool's biggest victory?

4. Which country defeated Sadio Mané's Senegal at the African Cup of Nations?

5. At which ground did Liverpool suffer their first defeat?

Ask Your Dad

6. By what name was the Kenny Dalglish Stand originally known?

7. Who were the visitors to Anfield for the last game played in front of the standing Kop?

8. In what year did Liverpool first wear a silver/grey away strip?

9. Who was Liverpool's last League title winning captain?

10. Which former Red played against Liverpool in the 1977 European Super Cup?

Fill In The Blanks

11. The first Brazilian to play for Liverpool was _____.

12. A badge first appeared on Liverpool's shirt in the 19__ FA Cup final.

13. When Liverpool last appeared in the Champions League they were in a group alongside FC Basel, _____ and Real Madrid.

14. Jürgen Klopp managed two teams prior to joining Liverpool, Borussia Dortmund and _____.

15. In the words of our famous anthem 'at the end of the storm there's a _____ sky'.

Name The Year…

16. Liverpool first won a European trophy?

17. Jordan Henderson was signed?

18. Anfield last staged an England international match?

19. Kenny Dalglish resigned as Liverpool manager?

20. Philippe Coutinho was born?

True Or False

21. Liverpool once played in blue and white shirts

22. Simon Mignolet is a Dutch international

23. Liverpool have won more European trophies than any other British club

24. Emre Can joined Liverpool from Bayer 04 Leverkusen

25. During his playing days Bill Shankly was a goalkeeper

Bonus Question

Which five teams did Liverpool beat en route to winning their first European Cup in 1977? (one point for each)

Answers on page 60 & 61.

Player Profiles

Adam Lallana
Midfielder
Squad Number: 20

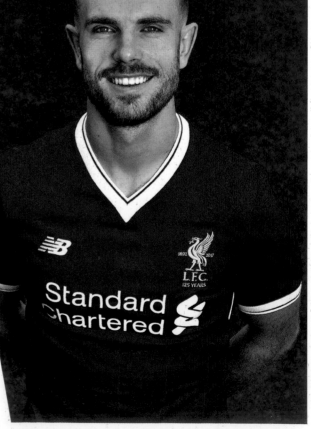

Jordan Henderson
Midfielder
Squad Number: 14

Philippe Coutinho

Midfielder

Squad Number: 10

Alex Oxlade-Chamberlain

Midfielder

Squad Number: 21

Reds in Europe

After just a one year absence, Liverpool Football Club is back in European competition for the 2017/18 season and many new adventures – hopefully happy ones – await.

Since the Reds first ventured competitively onto the continent in 1964 the club has played games in 37 different European countries (including England).

Have a look around this map of Europe to see where we've been…

NORWAY 2
- OSLO
- BERGEN

ICELAND
- REYKJAVIK

SCOTLAND 8
- GLASGOW (X4)
- EDINBURGH (X3)
- ABERDEEN

ENGLAND 10
- LEEDS
- LONDON (X7)
- NOTTINGHAM
- MANCHESTER

DENMARK 2
- ODENSE
- COPENHAGEN

NETHERLANDS 8
- ROTTERDAM
- AMSTERDAM (X2)
- ARNHEM
- EINDHOVEN (X3)
- UTRECHT

NORTHERN IRELAND 1
- BELFAST

IRELAND 2
- DUNDALK (X2)

WALES 1
- WREXHAM

BELGIUM 8
- BRUSSELS (X5)
- LIÈGE (X2)
- BRUGES

LUXEMBOURG 1
- ESCH-SUR-ALZETTE

FRANCE 17
- ST ÉTIENNE
- PARIS (X2)
- AUXERRE (X2)
- STRASBOURG
- MONACO (X3)
- BORDEAUX (X2)
- MARSEILLE (X3)
- TOULOUSE
- LYON
- LILLE

SPAIN 17
- BILBAO (X2)
- SAN SEBASTIÁN
- BARCELONA (X4)
- VALENCIA (X2)
- VIGO
- A CORUÑA
- SEVILLE
- MADRID (X4)
- VILLARREAL

PORTUGAL 10
- SETÚBAL
- LISBON (X5)
- PORTO (X3)
- BRAGA

SWEDEN 1
- MALMÖ

FINLAND 6
- OULU (X2)
- HELSINKI (X2)
- KOUVOLA
- LAHTI

RUSSIA 6
- MOSCOW (X3)
- VLADKAVKAZ
- SAINT PETERSBURG
- KAZAN

LITHUANIA 1
- KAUNAS

BELARUS 1
- GOMEL

GERMANY 19
COLOGNE
MUNICH (X4)
FRANKFURT
BERLIN
DRESDEN (X3)
MÖNCHENGLADBACH
HAMBURG
DUSSELDORF
DORTMUND (X3)
LEVERKUSEN (X2)
AUGSBURG

POLAND 3
- WROCŁAW
- ŁÓDŹ
- POZNAŃ

UKRAINE 2
- KIEV (X2)

CZECH REPUBLIC 2
- LIBEREC
- PRAGUE

SLOVAKIA 1
- KOŠICE

AUSTRIA 3
- VIENNA
- TIROL
- GRAZ

HUNGARY 5
- BUDAPEST (X5)

ROMANIA 7
- PLOIEŞTI
- BUCHAREST (X6)

GEORGIA 1
- TBILISI

SWITZERLAND 8
- GENEVA
- ZÜRICH
- SION (X2)
- BASEL (X3)
- BERN

SLOVENIA 1
- LJUBLJANA

BULGARIA 5
- SOFIA (X5)

SERBIA 1
- BELGRADE

MACEDONIA 1
- SKOPJE

TURKEY 7
- TRABZON (X2)
- ISTANBUL (X5)

ITALY 13
- MILAN (2)
- TURIN (X3)
- ROME (X4)
- GENOA
- FLORENCE
- NAPLES
- UDINE

GREECE 5
- ATHENS (X5)

CYPRUS 1
- LIMASSOL

Adam Lallana: Mind, Body and Soul

How do different parts of the human body contribute to the make-up of an elite footballer and how do they affect his performance on the pitch? Liverpool and England midfielder Adam Lallana calls on his own personal experiences in an attempt to explain…

Brain

"As my career has progressed, I've become more aware that mentality in football can actually be more important than the physical and technical parts, especially the higher up I've played. The older I've become, the more I've appreciated the mental side of the game and its impact. Playing two games in less than 48 hours (against Manchester City and Sunderland in 2016/17) was as much about mentality as anything else. After the City game, we were all exhausted and it was a tough game to see out mentally; they had a lot of the ball and so to then have to go again two days later, people were saying it would be physically difficult. But the brain is such a powerful tool and you tell yourself you're going to be alright. You tell yourself you've got another game in two days' time and that you'll be fine and it's amazing what your body can do. That is mental strength summed up for me."

Ears

"Communication on the pitch is vital, even if it's just one or two words to your teammate. It is difficult to be able to listen to each other during games due to the noise sometimes. As well as that, when you're tired in games, trying to get a full sentence out is sometimes difficult. Sometimes it can just be a scream of 'left', 'right', 'I'm on' or 'man on' – just these simple, simple words can mean an awful lot and help an awful lot. If you're covering your mate, you just want to shout 'left, left' rather than a full-on sentence, which is impossible during a match anyway. Maybe when someone is down injured or there's a substitution, you might be able to have a little bit of a conversation, but sometimes these messages can be so short. However, as a player, you know what they mean and something as simple as one or two words can mean an awful lot."

Eyes

"Vision and awareness is so, so important during games. It's big. The manager speaks about that all the time – about orientation and looking over your shoulder. In the position I have found myself this year, I am learning even more about how important it is to be 'orientated', which is the word the manager uses. Obviously you haven't got eyes in the back of your head, so to keep checking over your shoulders and knowing what is around you is so, so important."

Mouth

"Open communication happens daily here at Melwood. It comes from the manager – that's where his quality in his man-management comes out. Sometimes he will grab someone for a conversation in the warm-up or after training, or sometimes he might call people to his office depending on what issues are relevant at the time. He is very approachable and he's said from day one his door is always open, but it's important that you don't always go to him for everything – he probably has got enough on his plate and enough decisions to make! His assistants are vital – Zeljko and Pete – and Pep [Lijnders] is there if you ever need to speak about any matters as well. There's also the medical team, who you can speak to, and even in the gym, there are people there from the sports science department. It's important you don't speak to the manager for every issue – there are other people here you can speak to about different issues."

Heart

"Never being prepared to give up on a game can get you over the line. The Dortmund game springs to mind straight away. From the early days when the manager came in, he would turn around to the crowd and get them to keep supporting the lads right until the end. The matches last for 95 or more minutes now. I think it was West Brom at home when Divock scored [an equaliser] in the last minute, that came off the back of the manager getting the crowd going. If I've seen anyone believe and keep fighting right until the last minute, it is the manager. He certainly doesn't let us stop believing until the final whistle has been blown."

Stomach

"I can't stress enough how important nutrition is in football. Again, looking back to the two games in 44 hours at the turn of the year, we literally got into the dressing room after the City game and had a plate of pasta. Getting home, I ate another big plate of pasta and some meat. The next day, it was about eating all day, as often and as much as possible really. I think I woke up about 7.45am and had toast in bed. Then about 10 o'clock, I had some Weetabix with banana. At midday, I had two bacon and egg sandwiches in a bap. I got into training at 3pm and had yoghurt and a Ryvita-type bread with chicken and a shake. We did recovery and then after that, I had pasta, chicken and veg. We travelled to Sunderland, got there about 8.30pm at night and I had two big sandwiches, packed with meat, and yoghurt. The next day, on the morning of the game, you eat as much as you can. Fluids also work alongside nutrition; they both go hand-in-hand. It's important to be hydrated all the time and we have different supplements and drinks pre-match, different electrolytes. Shakes after games are very fruit-based; we have smoothies with proteins in them. Replenishing everything you've lost is so vitally important."

Legs

"Your mentality can have a positive impact on your stamina. How did I run more at Sunderland than against Manchester City? It's just the mental side of it, probably.

I went into that Sunderland game knowing I was ready to play – we all did. The manager said to us on the morning that we were physically ready for that battle – and we showed we were. It's possible I may be fitter now than what I was a year ago, who knows? I am just doing what I get told to training-wise and we're a fit team, it's not just me. We do run a lot and a lot of the time we do run more than the opposition – maybe that coincides with the manager's style of play. It's probably a side of my game I've had to adapt, but that's from learning from him."

Feet

"I've always worked off both feet for as long as I can remember, really. I can remember my dad used to encourage me to practise with my left as well as my right. I've always been renowned for being comfortable with my weaker foot – and that's always been very useful for me. Maybe I don't really see it as being such a big thing because I am just used to playing off both feet, although I do feel it is important and do feel it gives me an advantage. I'd like to think I've always been blessed with quick feet too. I think I have always had it – I always remember people at school saying I had good feet. I might not have been the quickest or the biggest, but I used to get away with it – 'He's got quick feet, he gets out of sticky areas with the ball'. That's a strength of mine I've probably had throughout my career and luckily enough I've still got it now."

And finally...

"It's not just a cliché, fans really can make a difference. The supporters can impact a game probably more than they can imagine, honestly. When the crowd are singing, they're up and in that good mood, you really do feel it out there on the pitch. It lifts you personally, us as a team and does make a difference."

Mr Liverpool:
A Tribute to Ronnie Moran

The term 'legend' is one that is often overused in footballing parlance but when it comes to the late, great Ronnie Moran there can be no more apt description…

The trophy haul says it all. In his 49 years at Liverpool Football Club, Ronnie Moran was instrumental in the lifting of 13 League Championships, four European Cups, two UEFA Cups, five FA Cups and five League Cups.

As a former player, captain, coach and caretaker manager Moran saw it all and did it all – most famously as an integral member of the legendary Boot Room, the inner sanctum established by Bill Shankly and maintained through the managerial reigns of Bob Paisley and Joe Fagan.

His coaching career continued under Kenny Dalglish, Graeme Souness and Roy Evans – happy to be the number two – Moran was revered as one of the most successful and respected coaches in the history of English football.

Born in Crosby in 1934, he signed professional forms for Liverpool, his home-town club shortly before his 18th birthday in January 1952.

R.I.P. Bugsy - You'll Never Walk Alone

In his career as a defender he made 379 appearances, scoring 17 goals and winning a Second Division championship medal in 1962. He only missed seven games when the First Division title was won two years later.

A robust left back, his enthusiasm for the game spread throughout the team. Such was his commitment and influence, as his playing career drew to a close, Bill Shankly invited him to join the backroom staff, launching a new chapter in the club's illustrious history.

Liverpool's Boot Room team, with Moran as a powerful voice in a tight knit group, plotted the downfall of England's and Europe's most famous clubs. Known affectionately as 'Bugsy', he demanded the highest standards – and any player found wanting was reminded of his responsibilities in no uncertain terms.

Players would come and go, managers would pass on the baton, but Ronnie Moran was a constant and the trophy cabinet at Anfield was testament to his genius.

Moran stepped into the role of caretaker manager on two occasions in the 1990s and proudly led the team out at Wembley for the 1992 FA Cup final against Sunderland.

When retirement came six years later, it marked the end of an era at Liverpool.

In March 2017, Moran sadly passed away following a short illness. He was 83 years of age. His passing was widely mourned but his achievements at Anfield will never be forgotten.

The legendary Ronnie Moran was, quite simply, Mr Liverpool.

Spot the Difference

Take a close look at the two pictures below and see if you can spot the 10 differences…

Answers on page 60 & 61.

Missing Men

Pictured below are four Liverpool teams, photographed prior to kick-off in their respective European finals. We've blanked out the faces of two players in each team, can you work out who they are?

1 1984 European Cup final v AS Roma – Stadio Olimpico, Rome

2 2001 UEFA Cup final v Alavés – Westfalenstadion, Dortmund

3 2005 Champions League final v AC Milan – Atatürk Stadium, Istanbul

4 2016 Europa League final v Sevilla – St Jakob-Park, Basel

Answers on page 60 & 61.

Player Profiles

Mohamed Salah
Forward
Squad Number: 11

Roberto Firmino
Forward
Squad Number: 9

Sadio Mané

Forward

Squad Number: 19

Daniel Sturridge

Forward

Squad Number: 15

Meet The Team Behind The Team

The players and manager may represent the public face of the first team but the backroom staff who work behind the scenes perform a vitally important role too…

Željko Buvač
First assistant coach
Joined LFC: 2015

Peter Krawietz
Second assistant coach
Joined LFC: 2015

John Achterberg
First-team goalkeeping coach
Joined LFC: 2009

Pepijn Lijnders
First team development coach
Joined LFC: 2014

Andreas Kornmayer
Head of fitness & conditioning
Joined LFC: 2016

Conall Murtagh
Sports Scientist
Joined LFC: 2012

Paul Small
Masseur
Joined LFC: 2002

Lee Radcliffe
Kit management co-ordinator
Joined LFC: 2007

David Rydings
Strength & rehabilitation assistant
Joined LFC: 2011

Andy Renshaw
Head of physiotherapy
Joined LFC: 2009

Richie Partridge
Physiotherapist
Joined LFC: 2009

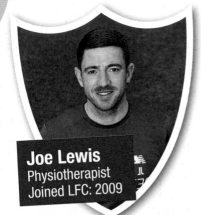

Joe Lewis
Physiotherapist
Joined LFC: 2009

Ruben Pons
Physiotherapist
Joined LFC: 2014

Matt Konopinski
Physiotherapist
Joined LFC: 2009

Mona Nemmer
Head of Nutrition
Joined LFC: 2016

Christopher Rohrbeck
First-team physiotherapist
Joined Liverpool: July 2017

Scott McAuley
Physiotherapist
Joined LFC: 2014

Greg Mathieson
Technical scout - Opposition
Joined LFC: 2015

Mark Leyland
First-team post-match analyst
Joined LFC: 2013

James French
Opposition analyst
Joined LFC: 2012

Graham Carter
Kit man/co-ordinator
Joined LFC: 1999

Quiz and Puzzle Answers

P36 Wordsearch

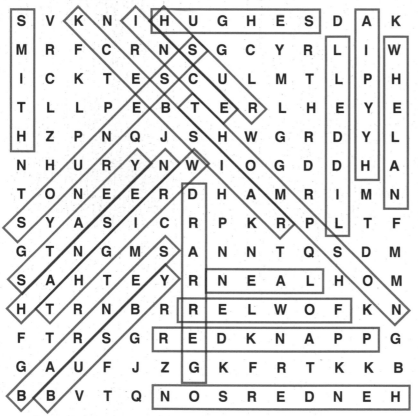

```
S V K N I H U G H E S D A K
M R F C R N S G C Y R L I W
I C K T E S C U L M T L P H
T L L P E B T E R L H E Y E
H Z P N Q J S H W G R D Y L
N H U R Y N W I O G D D H A
T O N E E R D H A M R I M N
S Y A S I C R P K R P L T F
G T N G M S A N N T Q S D M
S A H T E Y R N E A L H O M
H T R N B R R E L W O F K N
F T R S G R E D K N A P P G
G A U F J Z G K F R T K K B
B B V T Q N O S R E D N E H
```

P43 Quiz is Anfield

1. Leeds United
2. Steven Gerrard
3. 6-1 v Watford
4. Cameroon
5. Turf Moor
6. Kemlyn Road
7. Norwich City

8. 1987
9. Alan Hansen
10. Kevin Keegan
11. Fabio Aurelio
12. 50
13. Ludogorets
14. Mainz

15. Golden
16. 1973
17. 2011
18. 2006
19. 1991
20. 1992
21. True

22. False
23. True
24. True
25. False

Bonus: Crusaders, Trabzonspor, St Étienne, FC Zürich, Borussia Mönchengladbach

P54 Spot the Difference

P55 Missing Men

1. 1984 European Cup final v AS Roma – Stadio Olimpico, Rome

   Whelan (front row first from the right) & Johnston (front row second from the right)

2. 2001 UEFA Cup final v Alavés – Westfalenstadion, Dortmund

   Hamann (back row first from the right) & Owen (front row first from the left)

3. 2005 Champions League final v AC Milan – Atatürk Stadium, Istanbul

   Carragher (back row second from the right) & Finnan (front row first from the left)

4. 2016 Europa League final v Sevilla – St Jakob-Park, Basel

   front row Milner (middle) & Coutinho (front row second from right)

Where's Mighty Red?